Traveling Mercies

poems by David Williams

Alice James Books
Cambridge, Massachusetts

Library of Congress Cataloging-in-Publication Data

Williams, David, 1953 June 18-
  Traveling Mercies : poems / by David Williams
  p. ; cm.
  ISBN 0-914086-98-7 :
  1. Lebanese Americans--Poetry. I. Title.
PS3573.I44844T7 1993
811'.54--dc20   92-38738
                                                CIP

Cover photo by the author.

Special thanks to Martín Espada, Chris Gilbert, Lynn Gostyla,
Lawrence Joseph, Lisa Suhair Majaj, Lance McKee, Naomi Shihab
Nye, Cheryl Savageau, Fran Quinn, and Manuel Zax.

The author is grateful for a 1984 fellowship from the
Massachusetts Council for the Arts.

Alice James Books gratefully acknowledges support from the
National Endowment for the Arts and from the Massachusetts
Cultural Council, a state agency whose funds are recommended by
the Governor and appropriated by the State Legislature.

Alice James Books are published by the Alice James Poetry
Cooperative, Inc. Alice James books, 33 Richdale Avenue,
Cambridge, Massachusetts 02140.

Grateful acknowledgement to the editors of the following, in which
some of these poems first appeared:

America: Homage to Oscar Romero
The Amicus Journal: Outdoor Movies at the State Park
The Atlantic: In Praise of the Potato, Privacy
Beloit Poetry Journal: Keeping Watch, The Violin Maker
Equinox: Lasts
Harbor Review: Security Forces
Hayden's Ferry Review: Pueblo Day School
Kenyon Review: Come down with me from Lebanon
The Little Apple: After Banking Hours, In Memory of Maura Clarke
and All the Others
Michigan Quarterly Review: Almost One
Mr. Cogito: A Mirror in the Karentina, Seeds and Names
Paintbrush: Available Light
Poetry East: Breath, My Great-Uncle's Broken Song, In Memory,
Constellations, Río Escondido, Further Arguments Against the War,
Collusion, In Exile
Sierra: Ecology
Sonora Review: Bright Weight and Sight
Worcester Review: After the Sumpul Massacre
Poetry from the Amicus Journal (anthology): Outdoor Movies at the
State Park

Contents

Recognition 1

These poems are for the people in them.

Recognition

for Lynn

You taught me the names of trees I'd known
only as a lyric blur
of leaves turning up their pale undersides
in wind that made me speak
of flames and tongues.

"Saw-toothed" or "heart-shaped" the field guide says,
but your recognition is quicker
than even the breathless space between
two words. You join the leaf
flying on its stem.

I.

Breath

The people I come from were thrown away
as if they were nothing, whatever they might have
said become stone, beyond human patience,
except for the songs. But what is their daily
breath against all the the ardent, cunning
justifications for murder?

The stunned drone of grief becomes the fierce,
tender undertone that bears up the world,

steady as a river grinding soil out of stone.
I'm thirsty for words to join that song –
cupped hands at the spring, a cup of
rain passed hand to hand, rain pooled
on stone, a living jewel, a clear
lens trembling with our breath.

My Grandmother and the Dirbakeh

in memory of Mary Joseph Hashim

By tradition a man played that drum
while she set black olives, white cheese,
and the bread that wrapped them both
beside him. Cigarette ash

grew beneath his homesick grin
all through the song, but his hands
were possessed, faithful to the dance
till it ended. He knew the *dirbakeh*

wasn't his. He tightened and tuned
its slack face with gentle fingertip
swirls as he held it above
her stove, the same place she cooked

the lamb or fish whose skin would become
the new drumhead when this one broke.
He struck, and it answered – deep
at the center, bright at the rim –

and taught limits. Only the spirit
never tires, but hands can make it
resound. Try to feed off its blood,
and your jaws lock, bone against bone.

But surrender it your pulse
and generations link hands
in the dance and stamp the earth
to wake the dead. Though afterwards

he flicked his ash with an old pettiness,
and shrugged my grandmother's fingers
off his shoulder. Did his own hands
accuse him, swollen and sore

from pounding, when a light precise touch
would have drawn the resonant drum voice to flood
the emptiness like a spring?
Orphaned early, she was a woman who'd ask

almost everyone to her table. It's her
touch I want to bring to the drum,
playing steady past the erratic
heartbeat that couldn't sustain her

body. She used to pound grain
in the stone hollow of the *jrun*
with a pestle. That's my drumming,
she'd say drily. But I want to imagine

she played the *dirbakeh* when she was alone
with the memory of a long-dead aunt
who'd outlived any man
who could tell her what to do,

and so was free to prepare the waterpipe
like a tower from which to praise God,
balance the coals, draw the smoke through the well,
taste it, blow it out, and laugh.

Head o' Falls

At Head o' Falls, the tenements
were fragrant with onions and oil
though the ghosts of famine in Lebanon
hovered in kitchen steam.

The women walked home from the mill,
bits of wool still caught in their sweat,
and met an old Yankee whose pick-up truck
was loaded with cheap cuts of lamb.

They tried to make something whole
in the roundness of pots and plates,
each one feeling her own way through
while the river beyond the wall

kept its voice, bearing logs and suds
toward the coast. When it rolled below sleep,
constant as blood in their ears,
they flowed even further east

through torn, tearing names – Blessed Virgin,
Astarte, Eve – to a grotto
in Lebanon, a spring
dedicated to a nameless source.

*

I made up the part about Astarte and that,
but the ghosts of famine are real.

There's always one more tough guy trying to
prove we're nothing but skin and bones.

Some people hunch, bitter, above their pain,
while others stand up raw

and tender in the wind
and see
        the family's huge.

*

My father and his brothers, that whole skinny bunch
of kids, jumped their sister's husband,
and told him if he ever beat her again,
that was it, make no mistake.

Aunt Mary hated fighting. She bowed
her head and prayed for them all.
Her love came down like the river,
burdened, self-cleansing, defenseless.

Her husband bought himself a pinky ring
and holed up with his collection
of 78's from Egypt. Those thick
black discs were his perfection.
God forbid anyone should touch them.

He wouldn't leave them when the river flooded.
To save his life, the boys had to drag him
cursing and squirming up the hill.
His records and gramophone floated
out the door and over the falls.

*

Imagine everyone who once lived around here
gathered back to these shunned streets!

They're dead and gone. The whole neighborhood's
paved over, a parking lot. That's that.

The earth bears our mark like an unnamed wound
denied and passed on for generations.

Well then maybe the trees absorbed their voices –
Ticonic, French, English, Arabic . . .

By the bridge I found a young weedy oak
hanging onto its pale brown leaves.

I wanted to say they were ancient parchment,
or newly-hatched butterflies drying their wings.

Instead I listen to them stirring,
singing the wind.

*

A tree, year by year, can draw old wounds
through its sweetwood into its dry strong heart.
You can see them, when the trunk's cut,
like stones in a cove, growth-ring ripples
breaking around them, the circle still whole.

Logs by the thousands were floated downriver.
Chained here waiting behind a boom,
they nodded and creaked and murmured like
deep woods in the current's wind

while Mary alone or in a circle of women
said the rosary. Their woes
were an ancient pattern of stones,

but a tide rose with their prayers, their boat
was lifted up, though God alone knows
what they threw over the side

before drifting free.

*

In Lebanon a village woman
might climb a steep mountainside barefoot
and hobble home tracking blood
to do penance for a too-proud man
or appease an airy lord

      but the Holy One
        the Holy One
        the Holy One wants something else.

*

Mary's large eyes seemed to grow larger
as sickness withered her body.
She nodded to death without fear
or hatred of this life.

I would gather her the wildflowers of this place
and the others whose absence marks
where the glacier scoured and gouged the land
and plowed their seeds far south,

dumping boulders at random along the coast
that fishermen out at sea
would fix on to make it home.
The ice melted, and the wound it left

became a river –
this Kennebec –
and rose with all the
waters of the earth.

Privacy

So what if I outsmarted a fish
I found beautiful and didn't need to eat?
The pickerel's mouth was around the hook –
one more instant he'd bite and be torn.
I jiggled a warning down the line,
and he backed off quick and smooth.

Across the pond a woman came down,
waded in so far and stopped,
but kept throwing out a stick
for her dog to return
while light off the water
dappled up her thighs.

She thought she was alone
so I turned away.

I remember how my father always entered the water
shyly, carefully wetting his skin
like a shepherd smearing an orphaned lamb
with another ewe's blood so she'd claim it.
Once he swam out so far alone, he didn't
know the way back when dark surprised him.
Then someone on shore he never met,
thinking of something else,
flicked on a light and he didn't drown.

A Tree by the Water / Saltatory Process

Say a nerve's a wire
insulated except for the nodes

between which electric messages leap
quick and sure as saltimbanques.

Unless, as in my father's case,
the insulation's been stripped

by an auto-immune response
nothing can reverse.

Then the impulse short-circuits,
and scales of plaque

block the dance of memory and name,
the pressure of thought remaining,

words fading away.

*

My father passing the window just now was
his father, the one I'm named for.
We resemble each other in all those things
the body saves or the child learns
without thinking, out of love.

We remind him of this or that every day,
but his longterm memory's good, and brings him
home to this world when he wakes up
lost in his own house.
It's that history I work to learn

again, the story a child loves
to hear but never quite understands,
hugging his father's voice into sleep,
never dreaming he'd have to imagine
what he might have said once he's gone.

*

I'm looking for my father in history
but accounts don't mention the kids
who brought bread and lentils and scallions
to the strikers. The photos are grainy,
each face reduced to basics,
sketched by shadows.

Shadows are all a camera saves.
Meaning's born from memory and faith
and presence. These faces will be
passed on, shadowed, illuminated,
altered by what we name them
and the current of our own quick flesh.

*

The Yankees laughed at the "stupid Frogs"
and "black Syrians" fighting each other
for weaver jobs at the mill.
Laughed that, not knowing English,
they didn't know the joke was on them.

But George Jabar and Bernie Ezhaya
had everyone down Head o' Falls
singing "We Shall Not Be Moved" –
after fifty years my father draws
their names and the song from thin air,

"a tree that's standing by the water."
In '34, textile workers struck
all over the country, most of Waterville
walked out, and before it was over,
the National Guard came to town.

But in the end there was a minimum wage
and a forty-hour week,
and a brief weave of song in English and French
and Arabic where, in another age,
the Indian village had stood.

*

I could go back where the Indian village
stood, but I don't know what prayer
can free the word the earth's
caught in its throat.

Dirty suds float downriver
like icebergs, nothing below.
A cormorant stretches its dinosaur neck
and glides the other way.

An English sparrow, one more exile,
lights in the brambles, but I can't find
the grapevine my grandfather planted
on this bank.

*

In the woods I come across
stone walls that marked the old
pastures, and an apple tree
still bearing the fruit of the Levant.

Unpruned, then abandoned, its strength's gone into
a lanky sweep of branches
while the apples are small as baby's fists.
Still they keep a tart sweetness.

No longer immigrant, seed remembers
how to be seed, branches retain
the ideograph of orchard
sprawled among maple and ash.

The body keeps faith with something
even stripping its own nerves.
A gesture, a glance, is passed on.
Blue shadows of Lebanese cedars

still move over us here,
currents of a distant sea
that take up what nerves
can no longer bear.

*

In Lebanon, as I write this,
people with nowhere to go
crowd along the Alawi River
and down to the edge of the sea,
hanging sheets here and there for shelter
and a gesture toward what's still theirs.
Children still splash in the water just to
do it, though parts of their souls have been burned
so deeply, they may never be soaked
all the way through again.

*

In Europe right after the war, my father
saw families of wandering saltimbanques
like blue flames in the shattered neighborhoods
drawing brief crowds as they leapt through impossible
instants of balance and touch.

So much goes along with us
on the border of vision,
"street arabs,"
orphans when we have no names
to bring them before our eyes.

The Violin Maker

From the heart of a hunk of maple he cuts
two thin slices, traces the classic
curves across their grain
with a finer saw, glues and clamps together
the back of a space that will resonate
violin.

Hidden in his steady hands
through cutting, sanding, gouging,
balancing, staining, carving,
is the curve of her ear where he tastes the sea,
the fiddler crab bowing the air with desire.

He polishes the face an extra time,
then touches it with a struck tuning fork.
The work is true. He smiles
as if his baby's exploring fingers
had uncurled the scrolls of his beard.

An old bow draws out the warmth of his hands,
tender as all his distances,
tones rippling out like growth-rings,
the fingerprints of God.

He sweeps up the sawdust and hangs up his tools.
Fiddleheads open in the marsh.

Outdoor Movies at the State Park

It's not that the people watching the movie
instead of the moon as it rises
over Lake Champlain have no souls.
It's just that in this expanse of water
and plain the glacier left
like a great calm after great suffering,
our eyes are drawn to any
bright flickering human thing.

That's why we kneel before charcoal grills
and offer our daily news.
That's why the children in their pastel clothes
seem to gather the last of the light to themselves
and give it back – voices bright, flickering.

Two orange life-jackets glow through the dusk –
father and daughter in a canoe
borne up by a transparent mystery.
In her eyes, he's a legend –
back straight, kneeling,
holding his paddle above the lake,
drops falling from the blade
like a blessing returned. He knows
they're safe now. Failure and compromise
don't matter until they reach shore.

Keeping Watch

All the time spring was coming on,
a machine drew her blood, spun the cells apart,
drained waste, gave back plasma, outsmarted
her body's defenses.
                 I covered her heart
with my hand and watched her pulse rate
beeping green on the monitor.

*

Side effects go through her body
like ages, generations –
bony, bloated, sometimes covered with hair –

while newspapers chanting place-names
into blank synonyms for agony
are pounded back to nothing in the rain.

*

With nothing to love you with
but this body that will die,
how can I trust things spinning
apart to fall together?

I look up. The air is alive
with winged seeds spinning beyond themselves
across maples already deepening
toward summer.

*

She says while we sleep
a woman comes
and sits by her bed till dawn.

Then we say her name all day long, a prayer,
keeping watch for eyes that know the face
we had before we were born.

After Banking Hours

After supper, two brothers split a pair
of red boxing gloves, and get their moves down
on the pre-fab wall of the branch bank
camped like a trailer in the vacant lot.

Their sisters keep jumping
and keep the rope rolling
over and under, quick in their wrists
and ankles and knees –
no place to rest.

A boy, head big as a flower pot,
looks out through tomato plants
crowded on the windowsill.

His mother, dizzy with kitchen steam,
steadies a baby on her hip,
listens to her daughters' feet coming down,
coming down, coming down,
coming down outside,
and calls to her husband

who leans out for a little air,
calmed by a furious cigarette
and *salsa* on the radio

and in their hips, like the island talk
that got them through the winter
and coaxes this humid, wrung-out day
toward rain.

In Praise of the Potato

Potato, sojourner north, first sprung
from the flanks of volcanos, plainspoken kin

to bright chili and deadly nightshade,
sleek eggplant and hairy tobacco,

we could live on you alone if we had to,
and scorched-earth marauders never bothered you much.

I love you because your body's a stem,
your eyes sprout, and you're not in the Bible,

and if we did not eat your strength,
you'd drive it up, into a flower.

The Loom

The radio says it's freezing tonight
in New Mexico. I imagine you
asleep there with your sisters,
curled and elbowed into their dreams.

Your mother pictures a spark flying up
the stovepipe, constellations, your father
driving away, cousins huddled
in a dead car on the flats.

She wants to bring them home as she gathers
children into her blankets –
from all over, whoever their folks might be,
till it seems like no one can breathe –

bodies still shielding the fire
at the heart of the four directions
as each day's unravelled and woven again
with the endless shuttle of waves.

*

These lines won't weave you a blanket
on the weft of falling snow.
When the cold woke you up, you'd been singing,
warm at the heart of the sky.

This morning there's water to draw
from under the mask of ice,
and a fire to stoke, and snow to melt,
and dry corn to boil plump again.

You lean by the stove till half the dreams
hunched last night stretch arms and legs
and arch their backs across your yawn
like a song sung cleaning ditches

for spring irrigation, sun in your bones,
and shafts of light across the weft
of rain on the loom of
sky and lake.

Pueblo Day School

Homesick for earth, I asked the children
to trace every coast on the globe with their fingers
and follow each great river back to its source.

Soon the world was spinning under our breath
as we called out every name we could touch
in that little room under the mountain.

Then "Can we art?" and they were drawing.
One of them paused, closed her eyes, crossed her arms
on her breast, and maybe went flying

to the mountain lake source of her river,
her secret name.
Eyes open, she drew a line, and I saw

the ice of her paper's blankness crack
and dissolve into living water
beneath her hand.

Bright Weight and Sight

I couldn't translate the Tiwa song
she sang to the pink armless doll she'd saved
from the dump. I didn't have a prayer

to save anyone, and felt like a lumbering
trespasser. Does the earth turn its back?
Whatever it was I'd meant to say

formed a body of dust and whirled off.
Oh sure, I could talk history
but that was no way through grief.

*

She's so light in her bones, she leapt
small bonfires Christmas Eve.
But when she tried to leap up into

her father's arms, he fell,
and staggered off beneath the weight
of the sky and his mute shame.

*

He didn't know what to surrender to,
a longing for fresh water from an ancient jar,
or whiskey. His daughter walked out of the eyes

of the plaza, and felt a wind that could knock her
down, and the breath inside her.
She remembered how he would steady his hands

on the irrigation gate,
so careful not to drown the young corn plants,
so careful not to waste water.

*

She looked past the village, the fields, the pastures,
the creek that connected them flowing out of sight,
the canyon expanding beyond any human echo.

*

Across so much still distance,
a human sound: her mother winnowing
corn: kernels in a round basket

tossed and caught, tossed and caught. The wind
takes the grit, but what carries life
falls back to the woven circle in her hands.

*

That kid likes to ride my shoulders,
leaning forward or back, to one side or the other
for balance, her bright weight and sight

steadying me through distances I can't name.
Sun chants off the peak, the windmill
creaks at the well. She touches down

lightly, and faces her village.
I head for town, but listen
for water swift under ice.

*

I saw her whirling on the frozen creek,
her fine black hair fanning out
the wingspan of stillness.

Sojourner's Air

A song goes out through the high clear air
in a high clear voice, wrapped round with the depth
of canyon and sky, heartwood surrounded
by growth-rings, the canyon with strata
of seas that came and went
like tides. Now swallows bank and loop
through ages, and nest in the cliffs.

The song glides with whirlpools swinging out
from each stroke of the oars.
Beyond the bay, the ocean floor suddenly
drops. Voices over the water

sound so close! The song has words –
tough apple buds
that open after a night of rain,
a place to sit, a welcome,
bread and honey on the table.

Ecology

Lovers with nowhere to go press against
dry tarry timbers in the dead silver mine
till the cold drives them out.
                                      A pack
of ski-doers give a starved herd of elk
a run for the money through deep soft snow.
Cheap kills, and the holiday's over.

The old man who lives beyond the mine
with a dog and radio, listening
to basketball back east,
heard a bear up a tree. Quick grabbed
his gun and shot him. Broke most every
branch coming down.
                                      No one to ask
why he'd done it, he hauled
the skin and meat
downmountain to the Chicana
with eight kids. No common
language – he couldn't explain.

He gathered the branches for the stove.

For My Grandmother

One of those small, sturdy women
scrounging kindling in the rocks

could be my *Sittoo*, who says for their sorrows
Haraam like an hourly prayer

some would translate *a shame, a pity*,
as if it meant nothing more.

*

Half-blind seamstress, never learned
to read, except the Novena booklet,
holiday cards, supermarket ads,

she reads futures in coffee grounds,
and we gather round with our cups.

She's afraid to look these days.
Too many deaths. Wait and see.
You'll know when the time comes.
That's enough.
Pray to the Blessed Mother.
God willing.

Her Brooklyn kitchen's in exile
from the mountain valley between
Jezzine and Sabah and the wispy
plunge of the waterfall there
shuddering like the silence
that follows the Song of Songs.

*

The time she died,
she looked down without pain
at her body on the table
and felt a little sad
the doctors called her back

to a world where bloody
sheets are hung out
like a flag of virtue,
Veronica's veil,

and her true name drifts
just out of hearing
waiting for Wisdom
and the Lord to touch
and lie down.

II.

Come down with me from Lebanon

And the ancient stones of our fathers
and reinforced concrete
both leapt like brazen calves at the will
of artillery, and knelt and fell
on the living and the dead.

I open my throat
with an old, ill-fitting
lament, and dig
for a face still whole,
a song great enough
to contain you all,
undertone spun out of molecules
of bedrock.

*

All the spices in the Song of Songs
kill no one, arm no one, and so
go unnoticed, bruised and fragrant
in sun-cracked stones underfoot.

Come down with me from Lebanon,
from Hanir and Harmon and the lion's lair.
Swallows hide in the face of the cliff,
gazelles browse in the lilies.

*

She's borne too many to fear death much.
The faces of every army that ever
broke itself on these mountains
are gentled in her children's faces.

She kneels before stone
with a grinding stone,
death's counterweight gagged
beneath her black dress,

and clothed in grief,
she draws the sun
as her hands raise domes
of bread on the coals.

*

Before eating, we blessed the hands
of our mothers and sisters, we inscribed the names
of our father on the cold smoky air
with the warmth of our breath.
But a stranger answered,
and sat in his place. Our names
could not be found in the lines of his palm,
nor that first stroke, the aleph,
curved and opening like a wing
to call forth its lover, the world.
We called you father, we asked for bread,
and you gave us a stone. Your name
began with the downstroke of tearing
hungrily into our flesh.

_____

The title is from <u>*The Song of Songs*</u>.

My Great-Uncle's Broken Song

Habeeb I sing, who freely chose
to live with the chickens
under the road.
Any cruel thing you carried
fell from your hands
when he held an egg,
hen-warm, to your cheek.

Being simple, he didn't understand
when artillery rattled his beautiful pullets
and they wouldn't lay. No angel blazed
through chinks in the coop
when the dark ignited. Vines curled away
in the heat, and grapes were crushed
but not for wine.

Shall I tell him when men
of means say the word,
the poor fall like their shadows,
and Lebanon withers
to a garden of martyrs,
nothing for the living
but stone and mist?

Habeeb I sing,
in a human voice,
that some wind might bring him
the sea again,
crystals of sea air
in all the
hidden places.

A Mirror in the Karentina

Beirut, 1976
after a photograph by Don McCullin

At this distance, the hands are helpless.
Maybe you could shout some basic words,
stretching them out till they break.

On her back, arms thrown out, she can almost touch
a puddle reflecting the sky
that filled her as she died. The only

other tenderness here
is a plant, looking crazy now,
on a balcony overhead.

Smoke hovers by the second-floor windows
and expands. Empty rooms expand
inside the people who used to live here

and the people who drove them out.
At the end of the street, a tree
emerges through the burnt cloud

as if through mist, still lovely as if
it could reach alive and unbroken
into heaven.

*

The boy closest to the body
still guards her, nervous, as if she might rise,
while the automatic suns itself
at ease against his palm.

Death has entered him, a bride.
The vengeance being prepared
will find a girl in another street
who hasn't yet heard the news.

The boy beside him plucks an oud,
its delicate face still warm
with a morning they've already splintered
and drunkenly fed to the fire.

The next boy, mocking, triumphant,
screams a song, *love* and *God* and *home*
a ragged wind wearing his throat away
long after his voice is gone.

The other three look tough, smug, lost.
They might have just won a game
and now have no way to fill the space
thinning out all around them

till only the war remains.

A Face

All of you are close and unknown
to me as the bones of my face.

So when I heard the cries for vengeance
contaminating grief,

I wanted to hug the earth
and sink and disappear.

Instead I cradle
this oud I can't play,

its face unvarnished so not to deaden
the subtlest resonance,

its neck unfretted so it can answer
any ripple between two banks.

Spirit still moves through the body,
Mother of Mercy!

Seeds and Names

Cedar cones open and drop sweet seeds
from their tongues like the names of God.

Old men finger their beads and repeat
the one name of God that still burns through their shock –

whole families gone, whole neighborhoods gone
and plowed over, arms blown off

flew up against desecration, the roots
of a great tree clawing the air.

Now the children's hair is falling out
to mark the absence trapped in them, mute.

Their mothers pour out a measure of lentils
for everyone there, and pour

an empty cup for those who are gone,
as if to write their names on the air.

They smooth each measure with their palms,
pick out gravel and stems,

and sweep it into the cooking pot
with an echoing clatter like the names of God.

(Lebanon)

Available Light

When I think of how you bled to death
during the siege of Beirut,
your face dissolves into grains of silver
bromide, rocks on the moon
we see as a human face.

*

There was a girl who spent the winter in bed
because she was hungry and had no shoes.
Her father painted flowers for her
on the wall. A man took her picture there
in the Warsaw Ghetto. Her image survives.

*

I pick you out among all the lost,
a Jew, an Arab, who both could have passed
for my daughters, your trace dark crystals
on a negative, breath on a mirror,
a steady, invisible light.

The central section refers to a photograph
by Roman Vishniac.

In Memory

So many are lost, unnamed,
unsanctified by memory,
the whole damn country could be a shrine.
Wounds become foundations,
massacre made sacred,
the ritual repeated
in a trance,
each time new dead.

Your old life is torn up
for bandages, but you
save a strip dangling threads
from before the war:

After work Shafiq liked to sit outside
and joke and drink, a dependable clown
acting out crazy stories.
Then a fierce grief would seize him,
he'd break into tears,
blind with some unnamed doom we couldn't
see or turn him from.
Maryam, his wife, a small woman
with steady grey-green eyes,
would come for him then, speaking too gently
for us to hear, till his great heaving shoulders
grew quiet, and she guided him home
to bed. I don't know how it was
for her and the kids. With us she was friendly,
but dry, ironic, taciturn.

By day he drove a truck through the mountains,
linking the towns in a story, delivering
araq. You could drink it straight,
a clear anise flame, or milky
cut with water. He cursed the road,
but loved people gathered under an arbor,
the *briq* tipped to each mouth in turn
without touching the lips, a way to tell stories

that made the groves of olive and lemon
stand out, wheat and barley trembling
like a lover in the sun,
asphodel, anemone, cyclamen, flax
overcoming, in their season, the rocks.

In the high places there were shrines,
trees tied with bits of clothing from the
sick in hopes of a cure,
tombs of holy women and men
whose names had been long forgotten,
but whom Christian, Muslim, Druse
could all revere.

But the land had been broken up long ago.
You'd have to scramble and trudge for miles
to link the scattered terraces
of grain. There were schemes and torpor
in the capitals, big money
in Beirut, and refugees all the way
south to Reshidiyeh.
An old story. The nightmare explained
still recurs. The rivers here expose
no deeper strata, but ancient pavement
as they pound, silted red, to the sea.

Then the war broke open and would not end.
Shafiq went out to find his family
bread, and was killed by a sniper.
By someone's son, blind drunk with a vision
of pure fire, or a bored hatred
for anything that moved.

These days no one can give me news
of Maryam and the children
except that they're living in a mountain
village of no strategic
importance, where every street
is steep, each day's a climb

up and down, and the
angelic roar
of the falls across the valley
can't reach their ears.
No one knows them
at the roadblock a ways below
where the soldiers demanding
you prove who you are
change with the latest ceasefire
or alliance.

But this is a strip of story
tied to a tree. I'm telling you someone
still remembers where the old springs are,
and can lay down stones to guide a runnel
that will link the terraced crops.

No, listen, this is a crazy faith
in the way rain slips between paving stones
and finds crevices in rocks,
and reaches a grotto as clear, cool drops
a woman with steady eyes
touches for a blessing to her breasts.

Offering

Nights on the way to somewhere else,
so deep in the country the moon comes up
shucked free of any language, throws down
shadows and keeps rising
on the way to somewhere else,

I've wanted to speak with the faith of a man
who has always lived by the sea
and thrown out his net at dawn and returned
with something to offer. Around me now,
voices breathe in the dark

like waves beneath the tired complaint
of motor and gears. We stop. Then treefrogs
pierce the bus with their voices,
tossing their tight-lipped longing
back and forth in their swollen throats.

A grounded boat is freed on the incoming
tide, but I can't reach it yet.
The dead crowd in, and stretch out their hands
without a word. What can I give them?
In my dream she was still alive. I knew

her eyes again, her quick weight and heat,
and didn't want to wake up and see the dawn
expand. I would have stayed on
in the weeds by the side of the road,
blown back by the irregular pulse

of traffic, not to leave her.
But the days in which she is not on earth
also rise in these tassles and seeds.
When the dead stretch out their hands, it's not
to ask us for anything.

They know more than we what the living can give
one another, and don't want it paid to death.
They sway like underwater plants,
rooted by tide and moon,
and draw us on our way to somewhere else.

After the Market

Linger in the market
after it closes, the flash and tedium
of commerce done for the day,
a pouch of coins secure between folds
of a dress, goods rolled in a blanket,
whatever was feared or hoped for
come to pass.

To forget their hunger, kids play
hide-and-seek between the
stripped-down stalls.
Unsold weaving's laid out in the empty
plaza to be bundled,
and for a moment Rabbit, Bird,
Flower, Sun, Human, Frog

supplant the geometry of cobbles
while the women who brought those
bright shapes forth
through the tensions of the loom
discuss arthritis, the cost of yarn and rice,
marriages, funerals, fieldwork,
births, and busfare home.

Street musicians can finally let
guitar and trumpet sleep
in their laps, or play an extra riff
for free, out of joy or loneliness,
or some momentum still in their fingers,
or to close a curtain of privacy
around them.

(*Mexico*)

Mantle of Light

She might have passed unnoticed
but for the languid way she moved –
her dream her own, the air itself
open to receive her.

We were crowded together
on a second-class bus
lurching through the mountains
of Oaxaca, asleep on our feet

in the aisles, and still we made room –
God knows how – for whoever stepped
out of the dark at any crossroads
and climbed aboard.

The dawn grew around the big blue roses
printed on her satiny dress –
no help for the cold – and the hotel towel
she flourished into a shawl.

Still new to her womanhood,
she brushed against so much
that could break her without a thought,
we held our breaths.

And held her in our eyes
when she got off with some kid
a lot of us hoped was her brother,
and walked toward her village stiff

from standing so many hours,
and was gone.

And the women watched her most sadly,
knowing it wouldn't take much –
a drunk who didn't know his own strength,
a hemorrhage in childbirth, hunger

chewing her down one too many times,
envy, boredom, shame and the oldest
trick in the book at the edge of some dusty
town where there should have been jobs,

her own aspirations gagging
like a lamp going black with smoke.
A woman can take up a radiance
from the mute longing all around her,

and a man thinks he can grasp it
with the emptiness in his hands,
and falls on her, can't even see her,
knocks her down.
                    But at least that day
we stood back, our shadows cast
behind us, and let the flame breathe.
And how many, let out on the desolate road,

surrounded by so much
that could break them without a thought,
still guarded the bright space she'd made
till the air received them too?

Constellations

At night out here, the only human lights
are charcoalmakers' fires.
They're too far apart to trace constellations
between them. Each man works alone
to save what will go on burning
after everything burns away.

Hunger weighs nothing but it always swings him
up on the market scales.
So he works all night in the moonless sky.
His muscles know how many bundles of sticks
make one sack of coals to bring home.
In town he has a face again,

and debts. He turns from the sun and sleeps.
Cooking, we blow on knots of his darkness,
look up at a man nailed to the sky,
fire in every joint.
He longs to return, breathe on his hands,
hear the words: Come in, warm yourself, eat.

(Mexico)

Homage to Oscar Romero

Archbishop of San Salvador
assassinated 1980

Considered at first
otherworldly – safe –

he found, death by death,
the distance closing

between this life
and the one to come.

He became himself – *This is*
my body – became them all.

He said the simple, impossible thing:
In God's name, stop the repression!

He held up bread and wine
with steady hands.

The harvest comes
because the grain of wheat dies.

The vessel was broken,
but not one drop was lost.

In Memory of Maura Clarke and All the Others

I know how they left your bodies, Maura,
but tell me there's a secret body of light
they couldn't touch in you, that you touched
in the children you picked up along the road
too starved and shocked to speak.

I want the crystals of snow falling fat
and blinding on Guadalupe's feast
to open like roses. I want your vision
of wholeness reflected back
off broken faces.
                    The waters
can only come down and bear us.
That's their way. We look at our hands and find
arks of mercy beyond any shore.

_____

Maura Clarke was one of four North American
Churchwomen murdered in El Salvador
in December, 1980.

The Feast of Our Lady of Guadalupe is December 12.

After the Sumpul Massacre

1980

And when it was done,
and the banks of the Sumpul
blackened with carrion birds,

boys in uniform on the Honduras side
who had pushed the refugees back
into the river denied any part
in the killing, while on the Salvador side,
officers called it a Clean-up.

This woman defies them. She floated
unnoticed among the dead.
Her dead. They saved her. She saves
how the soldiers hacked into them screaming
Where are the guns? The guerrillas?

She hides them when she plants
by the moon's dark face
and bows the heads of ripe corn
to keep the birds off.
Good soldiers forget

dismembered bodies
rising through dreams
to breathe *I am you* without voices,
but fishermen's nets downriver
catch pieces of children.

She remembers how they turned
toward their names when she called.
No threat can silence her now.

Security Forces

The door-gunner may be a boy from the village
who wanted proof he was good and tough,
a uniform to hide his stringy muscles,
regular meals.

He couldn't hear himself wake up screaming
in the engine noise, amazed at the hate
he kept squeezing out of the automatic
as if the generals were dreaming him,
his own nerves turned away like grass
driven back by the chopper blades.

New he'll call it duty, believe it,
track everyone who might know him
just to prove he had no choice.

But if the wind's right, survivors hear
his rotors before he can spot them
sloshing and scrambling into shadows,
leaves, rocks, cliffs on the bank.
After he's gone, they wade out to pass
the children across over their heads

while just out of sight, he hovers above
an earth that does not know him.

Río Escondido

Sound of another boat –
I look up –
just our echo off giant trees.
Contras hitting the northern frontier,
rumors of contras south,
militia move behind branches
where pirates used to hide.
Men in the stern smoke and play cards,
engine too loud to talk.
Fighting cock tied in a sack on deck,
woman with the weight of her husband's head
in her lap, the freighter *Euroark*
out of Panama stalled in the channel,
our wake rolling out, jostling canoes,
washing the bank, drawing children
to the doorways of *chozos*
to watch us pass,
so close we'd just have to
lean over the rail
into the air
to touch them.

(1982)

Further Arguments Against the War

In a time of visions,
common things shine
like a newborn named Noah
or pictographs
washed up on broken stones.
Around Matagalpa, the midwives say
a woman is never more open
than after a birth. They lay on hands
down all her length
to close her.
Then she can rise.

(Nicaragua, 1982)

Collusion

Art and love require
particulars, but I speak
generally, emblematically,
because the story is not uncommon,
and too many details may identify
survivors to authorities,
and suggest the killers acted
with an individual flair –
almost artists, whose work
has been known to exert
a certain fascination.

Besides, I don't want
what knowledge I have
of my friend to become a story
that dies on the air when no one knows
what to say, or gets reduced
to a standard-issue poster
for quick and easy duplication,
generalized, disembodied,
like the President's voice on the radio –
no heat-lightning crackle
where life slips through.

But since the story is so common,
and we all begin to resemble each other
when our faces collapse in agony,
my evasions collapse. The *Guardia* took
her son up in a Huey
for questioning. The fact
that he knew nothing was irrelevant –
they had a point to make,
and threw his body, and then his head
out the door of the chopper
with the scraps of their lunch.

When her hands fly up
to cover her face,
the earth meets his body again,
their pain flares in our northern skies
a distended instant, exposing us
in a free-fall,
weightless as paper,
acrobats
who explain and deny,
explain and deny
till we hit the ground.

A Silence

Antonio:

How can a man be a man? You can't
defend your home, you have to
run. Then if you're lucky,
and the coyote doesn't leave you to
the desert or *la migra*,
you try to make enough
to keep your family going,
and send for them one by one.

And which one do you choose,
knowing how the soldiers eye
your daughters and remark
that soon your sons will be
of age to serve?

So you work double shifts whenever you can.
Send for your wife, and she gets three jobs,
cleaning offices and shopping malls
at night, afraid to sleep,
and houses in the suburbs afternoons,
both of you hoping the *nervios*
don't get so bad you break.

The *curandera* back home would know
what herbs might help,
but nothing grows here
except liquor stores and fools
in the vacant lot selling pills.

I try to comfort Lucia, but I
don't know what to say, and get mad
she can go out and make money
while I sit here and stare at my hands.

Last night I drank rum with the guys
and they talked all ashamed about fourteen-year-old
girls fighting as guerillas,
and vowed to return and end this goddamn war.

I didn't say anything. Knew today
I'd see them going to work,
keeping their mouths shut, afraid of informers,
afraid of *la migra*, glad the boss
would swear we're Puerto Ricans

while a jaguar goes on tearing at our guts.

I don't say anything, but I curse myself
for not bringing my youngest son sooner.
José Antonio – the poor kid's got my name –
crossed the border a month ago,
and he still won't talk. He's afraid to sleep,
hates to get up, but whenever he starts
to dream, the soldiers return and repeat
things he can't stand to describe.
He's scared to go out,
wants to just pull down the
shades and watch TV.

Now the news comes on, and everyone strains
for a glimpse of home, afraid we'll see
our streets in flames . . . But no, it's just
the president, blameless and proud.

María Lucía:

The president's proud and blameless as God
and Antonio sits there ashamed he can't
remake the world. Me, I keep

my eyes on the work in front of me,
or else I'd never get through.
Tortillas warm on the gas stove flame.
I grab them quick so they don't burn
and I don't burn myself,
and flick them into a dishtowel
in a bowl, and cover them up
like round-faced babies. And don't think –
except for an instant, I can't help it –
of the baby who died on the hillside,
mi angelito – there was no medicine,
my milk was no good, I was burning up
with fever, and fell on my hands and knees
between the coffee plants, the red beans I'd picked
spilling out and rolling away.
In those days we were always packed
in the back of some truck, getting bounced
from one harvest to another
all over the country. I only stayed
standing because of the people crushed in
around me. But now I keep my eyes
on the job. Time to drag my son
José Antonio out of bed.
All I do is work, all he does is
lie around, and underneath
the same panic. At one of the houses
I clean, there's a boy who loves
gory movies and video games about war,
and draws lots of pictures of people
getting shot to pieces,
and laughs, like he made it all up.
And José Antonio can't even tell us
what happened! When his father goes down
in that silence, I want to shake him
back to life, or pull him up
to dance like we used to do.
But who dares whirl or turn when the memories
of killers and victims might press in
on every side? I keep my eyes
straight ahead, on the ones who need me.

It's almost a relief sometimes
to go back out to work at night.
Cleaning offices we're mostly people
from places where there's trouble –
El Salvador, Guatemala, Mexico,
Haiti, Vietnam, Alabama,
Puerto Rico – it's like the real news
slips into the building after hours.
You look out the window on the 15th floor
and feel like you're standing in a cold silent sky
but no one can see you. The window's a one-way
mirror. Then all that space presses in,
all the time I was torn from my children
and Antonio. What do the new dead see,
rising from their bodies,
invisible to the helicopter
soldiers, who just keep
strafing? I want to be back
in this crowded apartment, eight people taking
turns in bathroom and kitchen,
the sweetcorn-and-ashes smell
of tortillas on the stove.
Then I look at José Antonio,
and my hands that are always full
feel empty. I want to sleep.
Sometimes when I can't take any more,
I dream of a woman in a *milpa* –
but only from the back.
It's beautiful. She wants to give me
something, but I wake up afraid
she'll turn and show me my face.

In Exile

Other refugees come to him
because he's been here longer
and will try to help them find a place
to sleep while the desert stretching
from both sides of the border
still glares inside them and
will not let them rest.

They love to repeat all the stories
of his close calls with *la migra* –
he's a champion bathroom window
fire escape artist.
But he's sick of it,
afraid next time
he might just give himself up.

In Salvador, he was poet, laborer,
organizer, preacher,
name on a death squad hit list,
too quick or lucky for random death.
He measures his life
by the dreams that bore him up –
the Gospel, new heaven, new earth,
revolution. And in each,
he found testimony – a poem –
and didn't go crazy.

In exile, all that mocks him.
Some days are so bad, he thinks:
Better to have been cut down
quickly, clutching a gun,
than to die here piece by piece.

He lies awake with everyone's voice
inside him, but can't write anymore.
Can't say he believes the war against those
who have nothing will ever end.
But he remembers bits of scripture and poems
prisoners repeat to themselves to go on,
and knows tomorrow he'll offer
what he can.
                    Leaning forward, listening,
his body forms a prayer he cannot hear.

Southside

Southside Presbyterian Church
Refugee Sanctuary, Tucson

And out in the desert, a dry wash flooded,
the tumbling current broke open
tough-shelled seeds, and now a young grove
of cottonwoods shades the bank.
When leaves stir, breath slips through
without documentation.

*

Some refugees, when they make it across
the desert and reach the church,
take the small statue by the door to show
the Virgin Mother of God,
and kneel to give her thanks for getting through.

But the statue's of a woman like themselves.
Her family was murdered.
She was left for dead.
Did God protect her?
God kept her alive.

*

Right before dawn, a breeze passes over
the people asleep or lying awake
in every corner of the church.
A stirring, a voice. Some have the faith
that offers words like breath.
They're like anyone – a crowd
could easily close around them –
yet each has seen the heart of the sun
unblinded, burning unconsumed,
and would make of immolation
illumination.

*

Others here turn over basic words
– *altar, blanket, cup* –
hoping their weight will hold them
to this world. Don't ask, don't ask,
but listen and abide.

*

At the altar, those who can write
write letters or take dictation
from the others. This man set his face
and tried to compose his life
in sentences that led one to the next.
He'd lived mostly in one valley,
and now, after so many borders,
and so many dry-mouthed nights afraid
his own breathing would betray him,
so many mornings his only thought
was *Figure out how to keep going*,
all he can manage to say is,
I got through.

*

But there are still prayers to greet
the morning star and the dawn
here and in the Maya highlands.

And the sun makes its way across continents,
unmindful of borders, once more tracing
invisible lines of connection.

*

Early morning by the church, the Maya
women are washing clothes
in an old bureau drawer. There's a sink
in the kitchen, but this way they
can keep one another company,
the rhythm of work their muscles know
so well almost lulling them home
for a moment. A loudspeaker crackles

English commands. The new people jump,
but the others explain it's just for the
garbage trucks at the waste treatment
plant up the hill.
                    Southside Tucson
can feel like south of the border.
The Border Patrol makes the rounds.
There are invisible lines here –
the old maps call it Papagoville,
and the Papago, who long before
named themselves *Tohono O'odham*,
still pray in the desert where outsiders see
just a bare ramada, a frame of sticks.

*

All the breath rising draws the light
on over us. Marisol
will tell you – though every telling burns –

she and her family pressed themselves
like nothing into the floor
to escape automatic fire.

Then they got up and dug the bullets
out of the wall, and carried them here
all the way from Guatemala.

Every night she dreams she's back home safe.
Then soldiers. She wakes up terrified
in the middle of our lives.

*

And out in the desert, a coyote paws down
through a dry wash bed for water,
and soon cactus wrens who nest among spines
come to drink, and elf owls who claim
old woodpecker holes in saguaros whose healed-
over wounds flame with honeybees.

Almost One

Airport security recognized my roots. The poor guy at the metal detector trembled and waved in reinforcements. I offered coins, keys, belt buckle, wanted to comfort them all, barely stifled a sudden longing to shout something Whitmanesque. My over-emotional nature inclines me to fanatical fantasies. I want to slip into terminals and depots, anywhere people wait hurriedly, neither here nor there, and seduce them into dancing in lines and circles that eventually join hands in one great spiral. Otherwise I'm afraid someday they might start screaming for blood, if only not to feel so small and alone. Such grandiosity and paranoia, not uncommon among my kind, is cancelled out by an equally characteristic fatalism, which leaves me speechless – a condition hard to spot among minorities, since we can barely get a word in edgewise. So many people can't wait to tell us, with a mathematician's pride, that they've got us figured out. Most generalizations, mine included, are blunt instruments, but some at least have the epic sweep of a memory ferociously repressed, or the momentum of the poor Legionaire in that long dying roll down a sand dune in *Beau Geste*. If I try to mention individuals – my cousins, for instance – are huddled defenseless at this very moment under an artillery duel in Beirut, the best of them might smile wanly and say, "It's been going on for two thousand years." But I understand. Who wouldn't pull back, if they could, from the chaos of grief? Exchanges with the dark ones carry risk. Ask the British. Ask the French. Among Arabs their soldiers found victory in places so extreme, they could never get home again, their businessmen cleaned up but lost their children in the desert, their academicians abandoned their meters to stalk malnourished boys, and to this day the sterile places grow. Rational men in the capitals of the practical can always accommodate a tyrant so long as he's only killing wogs. Then one day the anguish in the hollows and ghettos resounds in the finest districts, the flags unfurl, and everyone attributes their hatred to God. "Arabia" and "the West" keep bringing out the worst in each other, and what could save all our lives can barely be heard. And I, neither here nor there, got through the metal detector, with a double legacy and a double grief, the way, you might say, a camel carries water.

A Dream About My Grandfather's Life

in memory of Diyab Melhem

After even the wolf-cry dies away,
the stillness rising from the heart of the mountain
is everything – it includes the wind
in the trees below, and the trees stripped off

by armies long ago, and the trees to come.
At first there's terror, like the wolf-cry brings,
then the stillness is water transparent
and in motion, then you want to gather

rocks in a cairn for someone you'll never
meet, rest the lamb you came up here for
on your shoulders, its oily fleece
warming your neck, and make your way back

to the flock, your steps become quick and sure
knowing the loping wolf near.
Now you want to cut stones for a house,
build soil that will bear a garden,

pass on seed-corn light and dense
with reconciliation,
and a word that will do, something essential
your body wrote on the clear, fluid sky.

Lasts

Before the first big storm, I get out my old heavy boots. They're cold and stiff, a topographical map of last winter, but I put them on, and they start to soften up. I think of the shoemaker with his rows of lasts, all of us reduced to those few blunt shapes. I think of my mother heading back to the shoe factory the morning after her father told her, scholarship or no scholarship, girls didn't go to college. And I think of the stain going through her fingers, into her blood, and years later cancer. I can't help it, I think of the millions killed with no testament but their shoes tossed in a heap, and the others who, being barefoot, are even easier to forget. If I go on like this, I'll be struck dumb, but the news is full of rumors of war, conjured glories, willed amnesia, and I need to join with everyone trying to say something true. When I remember the Holy Innocents, I forget the Flight into Egypt. Three more refugees made it through the desert. I take off my boots and am pleased to find a little red dust hidden in the seams. I wore these boots in Chaco Canyon. Chaco! Imagine those cavalrymen a hundred years ago, confident the Union had been restored and the Navajo contained, snapping their reins, God's own vanguard in the wilderness. And then getting lost. And coming upon those ruins, older than anything they'd ever seen – whirling kivas, room leading on to room, cliffs full of voices and faces – out where they were positive nothing could live! Everyone I have ever touched has put more life in my hands, and entered my blood, and lit my brain, and even now moves my tongue to speak.

Glossary

Arabic

aleph – first letter of the Arabic and Hebrew alphabets

araq – anisette

briq – small jug with a spout

dirbakeh – Lebanese term for a small, chalice-shaped drum common in the Middle East

diyab – wolf

jrun – mortar

oud – stringed instrument, from which the lute was derived

Sittoo – (colloquial) Grandma

Spanish

curandera – traditional healer

Guardia – National Guard

milpa – (from Nahuatl) cornfield

migra – (colloquial) immigration authorities

nervios – (colloquial) "frayed nerves"; a condition marked by agitation, depression, and insomnia

Alice James Books has been publishing poetry since 1973. One of the few presses in the country that is run collectively, the cooperative selects manuscripts for publication, and the new authors become working members of the press. The poets are the publishers, participating in every aspect of book production, from design and editing to paste-up, from consultation with printers to distribution and marketing. The press was named for Alice James, sister of William and Henry, whose gift for writing was ignored and whose fine journal did not appear in print until after her death.

Recent titles:

Jeffrey Greene, *To the Left of the Worshiper*
Alice Jones, *The Knot*
Nancy Lagomarsino, *The Secretary Parables*
Timothy Liu, *Vox Angelica*
Suzanne Mattson, *Sea Level*
Cheryl Savageau, *Home Country*
Jean Valentine, *The River at Wolf*